Baby and Beyond

Progression in Play for Babies and Children

Bikes, Prams and Pushchairs

Baby and Beyond - Bikes, Prams and Pushchairs

ISBN 1-905019-76-9 • 978-1-905019-76-2

© Featherstone Education Ltd, 2007

Text © Sally Featherstone and Liz Williams, 2007; Illustrations © Martha Hardy, 2007; Series Editor, Sally Featherstone

First published in the UK, January 2007

'Baby and Beyond' is a trade mark of Featherstone Education Ltd

Published in the United Kingdom by

Featherstone Education Ltd, 44 - 46 High Street, Husbands Bosworth, Leicestershire, LE17 6LP

Printed in the UK on paper produced in the European Union from managed, sustainable forests

Contents

Baby and Beyond

A series of books for practitioners working with children from Birth to Three and beyond

This book gives ideas for introducing and extending construction activities and experiences for babies and young children. Each page spread contains a range of experiences and a selection of ideas for each of the four developmental stages of the Birth to Three Matters Framework, and extends this progression into the early Stepping Stones for the Foundation Stage:

Young Babies -
Heads Up, Lookers and Communicators
0-8 months

Babies -
Sitters, Standers and Explorers
8-18 months

Young Children -
Movers, Shakers and Players
18-24 months

Children -
Walkers, Talkers and Pretenders
24-36 months

Foundation Stage -
Yellow Stepping Stone and beyond
Foundation 1 and 2

Going on the bikes can be a real relief for many children, who spend too much time sitting down! From birth, boys in particular develop a love affair with wheeled toys of all sizes, which lasts a lifetime. Every setting spends money and time offering and organising bikes, prams, pushchairs and a wealth of other vehicles for the children, but there is often an assumption that these are just for unaccompanied, child initiated activities. However, with a bit of thought, practitioners will realise that there is much potential in using the wheeled toys at different levels for activities to suit different stages of development.

Even tiny babies can watch, wave at and learn the names of the toys, and as they get bigger, have little rides on them to get the feeling of movement. Older babies and young children will love to begin the process of learning to ride, balance, scoot, push, tip, fill, pull and empty barrows, trikes, scooters and other toys. This activity will help to develop strength and control in muscles and senses.

Later, children in the Foundation Stage will incorporate wheeled toys into their role play, developing different scenarios and characters who ride, deliver, collect, clean windows, paint houses, mend cars etc. Bikes and scooters become multi-purpose vehicles for endless play, and 'the best bike' is often a feature of a setting, undetectable by adults, but the focus of all attention to the children!

Adding simple props to the wheeled toys, will expand the opportunities for play - flags, streamers, baskets, bags, as well as hats, badges and tabards will all focus attention on group play, as well as extending the language and interactions.

Look at the range of wheeled toys in your setting and try to provide graded equipment to suit different stages of development as well as a wide range of different types of vehicles - scooters with different numbers of wheels, trucks and cars with trailers and containers, pushchairs for twins, bikes and trikes of all sorts and sizes to suit every child. Try to add some more unusual vehicles - some that need two people, some with hooks and hitches for trailers, some with no wheels, some for older children to scoot with their feet, rides for groups, Spacehoppers, pogo sticks, skates and skateboards, baby walkers etc. and keep some cheap sledges in reserve for the day when it suddenly snows!

This book will give you some starters and ideas for using the wheeled toys in your setting to support the development and creativity of all the children, whatever their age or gender.

p.s. don't forget to ask parents and friends for outgrown toys, you will often be surprised at people's generosity towards young children.

We have not suggested particular suppliers because there are so many, but one way to find unusual stuff is to put 'wheeled toys', 'balance toys' or other words in Google Images or another search engine to find hundreds of ideas.

Young babies (0-8 months)	Babies (8-18 months)	Young children (18-24 months)	Children (24-36 months)	Foundation 1&2 (over 3)

Heads Up, Lookers and Communicators	Sitters, Standers and Explorers	Movers, Shakers and Players	Walkers, Talkers and Pretenders	Moving on into the Foundation Stage

Going round

As a general introduction to bikes, prams and pushchairs, let babies and young children have lots of experience of things that go round and round and how wheels work. This experience should include handling round objects of different sizes and exploring what the children can do with them.

Young babies (0-8 months)

Introduce very young babies to circles through a wide range of experiences. Objects such as soothers or teething rings, rattles and baby gyms often include circular shapes to chew and handle. Putting things in their mouths is one of the earliest ways babies use to investigate objects. Clean plastic wheels from construction sets will also be used to bang, rattle, suck and wave.

Heads Up, Lookers and Communicators

Babies (8-18 months)

Babies will enjoy hangings and mobiles with circular shapes such as old CDs which sparkle as they turn in the wind and sun out of doors. Cups, plates, blocks, drums to feel with their hands, feet and fingers will increase their knowledge and experience of roundness, rolling and movement. Rolling toys, some with bells or objects inside will fascinate babies and encourage them to move as they follow the toy.

Sitters, Standers and Explorers

Young children (18-24 months)

Collect some of the individual pieces from construction systems such as Duplo, Sticklebricks, Briomec, Magnetic blocks, Mobilo, Gears. Play with them with the children, exploring ideas of rolling along and moving. Look carefully at the wheels on large small world vehicles, and spot wheels as you go on walks or visits and in the pictures in books. Read plenty of stories abut bikes, prams, cars and other things with wheels.

Movers, Shakers and Players

Children (24-36 months)

Continue to encourage children to look for wheels in the environment, on toys and in books and stories. Talk about the sizes and uses of wheels. Compare different wheels on the same vehicle – trikes, pushchairs, tractors, lorries have different sizes. Help them to build wheeled vehicles from different materials including construction sets and recycled materials.

Walkers, Talkers and Pretenders

Foundation 1&2 (over 3)

Develop obstacle courses with bricks, guttering, pipes, wood planks, large bricks, arches, tyres, crates, slides etc. for large and small wheeled toys to negotiate. Building vehicles from junk on large and small scale – Mobilo or Duplo, or use cardboard boxes, pram wheels, tubes and cable reels to make go carts and other models. Try to get vehicles to move without wheels and discuss why wheels are round.

Moving on into the Foundation Stage

Small push-along toys

There are many toys which can be used to introduce the idea of pushing objects along to babies and young children. They are made of both natural and man made materials, but natural are more suitable for very young children, as their colours, textures and scents are more soothing.

Young babies (0-8 months)

Simply holding push along toys and rolling them up and down familiar surfaces such as their legs and arms or someone else's arm, leg, or back! Help very young babies to explore the surface and shape of push along toys and thus the movement of them. Let the young babies follow the movement of the toy's wheels with their eyes as you push them along and talk to them about what is happening.

Heads Up, Lookers and Communicators

Babies (8-18 months)

Show the babies how the toys move when pushed, and help them to learn how to do it themselves. Letting go is often a problem, so you may need to push the toy towards the baby and help them to push it back over and over again. Eventually the babies will begin to push the toys back and will let go, just persevere! As the babies begin to crawl and balance they will be able to take the toy with them as they move.

Sitters, Standers and Explorers

10

Young children (18-24 months)

As they gain confidence and skill in their movements, young children will begin to make more complex games where they push toys alongside them as they move. Increase the range of toys to use for pushing to include larger scale small world cars, lorries, trains etc. Offer tubes and tunnels for the vehicles to roll through. This game will delight the children as the cars, buses and lorries disappear and appear again.

Movers, Shakers and Players

Children (24-36 months)

As children begin to interact with each other they will develop skills of pushing toys backwards and forwards between them. Extend this game by offering boxes, drainpipes or other containers to hide or put the toys in. Help them to take turns and play simple hiding and finding games. Encourage them to talk about what they are doing and seeing. Model 'Ready, Steady, Go!' or 'One, two, three, go!' to help with timing.

Walkers, Talkers and Pretenders

Foundation 1&2 (over 3)

Develop the play by working with a small group to compare how far different push alongs move. Explore whether it matters how hard or who pushes. Compare flat and sloping surfaces. Try different surface textures such as smooth floor, carpet, gravel, sand, tarmac, and how direction affects speed. Encourage the children to record their findings in pictures, photos, paint on tyres, dictaphones. Make a display or book of their findings.

Moving on into the Foundation Stage

Small pull-along toys

Pull-along toys can be used in two ways - to pull behind or to pull towards. Babies and children need to explore the difference between these two actions, as well as between toys you push and toys you pull. This all takes time and much practice but will include a great deal of fun along the way.

Young babies (0-8 months)

As young babies begin to focus with their eyes, or as an aid to help them develop the skill, you could move objects in front of them - towards them, away from them, across their field of vision. This tracking will help with focus and concentration, and is very good practice for babies when they are lying on their fronts.

Heads Up, Lookers and Communicators

Babies (8-18 months)

Babies who are beginning to sit will be able to grasp the string for a short while and pull it in a direction comfortable for them. This will usually be towards them, not behind them. Make sure the string is not too long, as this will be frustrating if they are not very mobile. When babies crawl, encourage them to pull the toys by tying the string loosely around their wrist so they can still use their palms for balance.

Sitters, Standers and Explorers

Young children (18-24 months)

By varying the toys available to them, encourage young children to pull toys both towards and behind them. Use ready made toys or make your own by by attaching different things to string, ribbon, rope, plastic springs from cheap keyrings, or sticks. Make some toys with wheels and some without. This will affect the ease with which they move as will the size and balance of the objects on the strings.

Movers, Shakers and Players

Children (24-36 months)

Children become more confident with walking and running at this age so they can pull at different speeds and in different directions. Help them to build obstacle courses for the children to negotiate the pull alongs around. Use bricks, furniture, big logs or cardboard boxes of different sizes and shapes. Add tunnels to crawl through and planks to walk along. Try the same obstacle course riding a trike and pulling a toy behind.

Walkers, Talkers and Pretenders

Foundation 1&2 (over 3)

Once they have had some practice, the children can make their own obstacle courses to see what will and will not work well with the objects. Give them some strings and let them tie their own objects on the ends. Use pull alongs in role play and link them with pulley systems outdoors, for instance in moving sand across a building site, or raising buckets to the top of a castle or climbing frame.

Moving on into the Foundation Stage

13

Large push-alongs & baby walkers

There is a mixture of large push along toys available some of which are an item such as an animal on wheels attached to a handle, others like a trolley with contents in it, formerly known as baby walkers. Each of these types can be used in a variety of ways with babies and young children.

Young babies can be introduced to larger push along toys by adults moving them within sight of the babies so that they can see and hear them. Put sound makers such as bells in them and they will turn toward the sound and follow it. Some baby walkers are big enough to sit a teddy or doll inside, and wheel it round the baby. Begin to model loading and unloading things in the baby walker.

Heads Up, Lookers and Communicators

Babies (8-18 months)

Introduce babies to the contents of baby walkers when they can sit unaided. Some baby walkers come complete with their own bricks and blocks, empty ones can be filled with toys, bricks, plastic cups, empty cartons. The babies can investigate the contents with all their senses – feeling, tasting, looking, smelling and hearing. Remember, putting things in their mouths is exploration, even though it can be a damp experience!

Sitters, Standers and Explorers

Young children (18-24 months)

As young children gain confidence in standing and stepping out, encourage them to walk, pushing the toy along in front of them. This will give them a sense of stability and security as they learn more about walking. The fun of a baby walker is that children can take a favourite toy with them as they venture out. Give them opportunities to use push-alongs and walkers on different surfaces indoors and out, up and down slopes.

Movers, Shakers and Players

Children (24-36 months)

Encourage children to use large push alongs in simple role play, moving things around or including the animals and other toys in pretend games. They could practice moving them along markings and roads on the floor inside and out. Loading and unloading objects will give hours of fun. Try offering real bricks, sand, cobbles and stones, specially to budding builders and constructors.

Walkers, Talkers and Pretenders

Foundation 1&2 (over 3)

Help the children to find ways of fixing the push-alongs to the backs or fronts of other wheeled toys so they can use them to carry loads. As the children move items around, see how many items they can put in before it is too heavy to push or pull. How many children are needed to move it? What will fit in the container and what won't? Can you take a friend for a ride? Can you use your new vehicle outside? How can you improve it?

Moving on into the Foundation Stage

Trikes

Tricycles are available in many different types and sizes, with and without pedals. Children will need to use their feet on the floor first to push the trike along without the pedals getting in the way. Some children will need a lot of practice at this before they will be able to use the pedals properly.

Young babies (0-8 months)

Once a young baby can support their own head, you could hold them in position on the smallest trike with a suitable seat where they will be comfortable. Spending time sitting with you, watching older children ride wheeled toys of all sorts will help babies to learn these skills. Watching a model is a key way of learning. The sensation of sitting astride something can also be practiced as you sing nursery rhymes with the young baby on your knee.

Heads Up, Lookers and Communicators

Babies (8-18 months)

As the baby becomes more confident and stronger, sit them on as appropriate sized tricycle and push them gently along. Choose the right size trike for the child - they need to be able to reach the handlebars as well as touch the ground with their feet. As babies become confident at walking they will begin to move the tricycle by themselves, scooting along the floor. This is easier indoors where the floors are flat and smooth, so make some space!

Sitters, Standers and Explorers

Young children (18-24 months)

At this stage, scooting along the ground will probably still be the preferred way of moving for most children. At first they will use both feet together, but as their coordination develops, alternate legs may be used. Once the children start to use alternate feet, you can offer small tricycles with pedals. Remember to check the seat to pedal distance - if it is too great the child will find it physically difficult to push the pedals.

Movers, Shakers and Players

Children (24-36 months)

Many children will continue to use their feet on the ground as a means of propulsion, at least some of the time, even when they have mastered pedalling, as they find it easier. Trikes with pedals on each side of the front wheel will affect the way the legs are stretched as they steer. Encourage children to steer the tricycles using the handlebars by drawing roadways with chalk or marking them with tape. Or ride through puddles and mud on wet days.

Walkers, Talkers and Pretenders

Foundation 1&2 (over 3)

If children are still having difficulty using pedals, talk to them about how they work and show them by moving them slowly with your hands. Use trikes, scooters and cars to make patterns on the ground in water, paint or mud. Try following each others' tracks and trails, or overlap them to make different weaving patterns. Fasten baskets and saddle bags to the trikes to encourage role play, and hitch trailers on for transporting objects.

Moving on into the Foundation Stage

17

Barrows

Wheelbarrows of all sorts and sizes deserve a place in every early years setting. As well as their use to transport endless numbers of objects, they can be used to encourage babies and young children to help with care of plants and the outdoor environment. They come in a range of sizes appropriate for all ages.

Young babies (0-8 months)

Very young babies can be introduced to the outdoors through transportation of different styles. If a young baby is being carried in a papoose-style sling by an adult they can watch the adult as they use a wheelbarrow, talking to the young baby as they work. Babies can lie or be propped on cushions in a barrow, watching the activities outside from a safe vantage point. Watch them carefully, sitting nearby to help if needed.

Heads Up, Lookers and Communicators

Babies (8-18 months)

Babies who are on the move will investigate anything that takes their interest. Put some tempting objects in a wheelbarrow so they can explore them, using the barrow to steady themselves by climbing up and feeling them. Simple piles of gravel, washed stones or sand will be enough, and they will provide some weight to steady the barrow. Babies may even climb into barrows if they are of an appropriate size. Remember to wash the babies afterwards if they have been outside.

Sitters, Standers and Explorers

Young children (18-24 months)

Some children will use a wheelbarrow as an aid to confidence on their feet once they have started walking, using it like a baby walker. Help them by putting well loved toys, soft toys or puppets in the wheelbarrow to be pushed or taken for a ride. Young children enjoy being your helpers so they can use their wheelbarrows for helping in the outdoors with gardening and carrying things. Offer some big wooden bricks for loading and unloading.

Movers, Shakers and Players

Children (24-36 months)

As children begin to develop role play encourage them to use the wheelbarrow for transporting sand, compost, bricks, tools, logs and other items. Make sure the contents are not too heavy for them to lift and push. Add a few builders' hats and work tabards, or green shirts and straw hats to enhance role play with tools and barrows. Some barrows are big enough for children to take each other for rides on grass or soft surfaces.

Walkers, Talkers and Pretenders

Foundation 1&2 (over 3)

Help children to develop spatial awareness by them pushing wheelbarrows along marked tracks chalked on the ground or made using masking tape. They can also make their own 'snail trails' by using paint or water on the wheel. This can lead to discussions as to where the start and finish points of a trail are after a child has left it. Encourage children to care for a small patch of garden and offer them real, but child sized garden tools and equipment which will include a bucket and a wheelbarrow.

Moving on into the Foundation Stage

19

Bikes

Remember that in order to ride a bicycle children need a good sense of balance. Most children will be able to ride without stabilisers by the end of Foundation Stage. There is a wide variety of bicycles on the market both with and without stabilisers for babies and young children.

Try www.cyclesense.co.uk for help and ideas.

Young babies (0-8 months)

Very young babies will be able to look at the different sections of bicycles with the assistance of adults. They can feel the spokes and the shapes of the wheels, handlebars and other parts, and be helped to investigate appropriate sized small world bicycles. Gently pushing a small trike backwards and forwards is a soothing way of exploring movement, and babies will reach out to do this given the chance.

Heads Up, Lookers and Communicators

Babies (8-18 months)

Older babies can sit in special seats attached to adult bicycles, where they will be introduced to the sensation of riding on one. Of course they must be harnessed in to the seat safely. See if a parent has one of these on a bike and can bring it to show your group. At this stage you can offer supported rides on small trikes to children if they wish, holding them and pushing them gently to get the feeling of riding and balancing.

Sitters, Standers and Explorers

Young children (18-24 months)

This is the age when children want to learn everything! They will start to push themselves along on bikes with and without pedals, and you may like to investigate some of the new bikes without pedals. Small bikes with stabilisers will encourage young children to begin propelling themselves, using their feet. Show them how to steer using the handlebars to turn right or left. They may find steering and scooting together difficult at first.

Movers, Shakers and Players

Children (24-36 months)

Using bicycles in role play situations, especially outdoors may include 'riding in role'. Delivering pizzas, cleaning windows, maintenance, post, TV mending, parcel delivery, police, petrol stations, rescue and many other roles will all give opportunities for riding and travelling on roads. Props, bags, tool belts, bike baskets and trailers will all encourage safe and stimulating play. Use large boxes to create tunnels and buildings and chalk to make roads.

Walkers, Talkers and Pretenders

Foundation 1&2 (over 3)

With practice, children will develop their own role play situations using bicycles, and will begin to introduce other dimensions, numbering bicycles and parking bays, using money for paying at the petrol station, linking the play to domestic or other themes. Older children will enjoy more grown up bikes with adjustable seats and without stabilisers. You may also like to add 'BMX' styles, motor bikes and mountain bikes to add variety and stimulate play.

Moving on into the Foundation Stage

21

Cars

Appropriate sized cars are good for extending development in several areas. They will help with gross motor skills as the children need to learn how to get in and out of them as well as how to move them, depending whether they have pedals or not. They also promote social development and cooperation in the use of space and negotiating with passengers.

Very young babies can be held by an adult to watch older children playing in and out of cars, even though they are probably not strong enough to be placed in a toy car for transporting. However they will react to the sounds of other children pushing horns and making noise as they move around. Tracking movement and is good training for focus and hearing. Sit them on your lap while you sing movement songs like 'The Wheels on The Bus'.

Heads Up, Lookers and Communicators

At this stage babies will be desperate to climb in to cars if they have open sides. They may need to be shown how to climb in and out most effectively as the coordination of the feet and legs may not be perfect! Once in the car they may spend long periods of time just sitting and exploring the steering wheel, turning it in both directions, or pressing the horn button. These first investigations are a vital stage in learning about a new activity, so be patient and let them have time.

Sitters, Standers and Explorers

Young children (18-24 months)

Climbing in and out will now have been mastered, and may become an activity in itself! Opening and closing the doors will be repeated again and again. Children may need help in moving the car, either by the adults pushing it, or by beginning to push it along with their feet on the ground. At this age, few children will be able to manage the pedals, but just moving the car along will give them a real sense of achievement.

Movers, Shakers and Players

Children (24-36 months)

As the children's muscle strength develops, they will become more proficient at moving the cars. This will include discovering which way to push their feet to go forwards and backwards. They will probably find it easier to move backwards as fewer parts of their legs need to work together for this. If this is the case, they may need to be shown how to go forwards and helped to practise this skill. At this stage, trailers and containers to pull are good additions

Walkers, Talkers and Pretenders

Foundation 1&2 (over 3)

Children will be more confident in handling cars and making them go where they want, so roadways marked with chalk, tape, cones, skipping ropes or bean bags can be offered to make routes more challenging. These can involve weaving in, out and round - excellent for spatial awareness. Children may also begin to use the cars to take other toys for rides. Role play garage scenarios can now be stocked with clipboards for check lists and car services, numbered bays and petrol pumps, or parcels and objects to deliver.

Moving on into the Foundation Stage

23

Pushchairs

Babies and young children enjoy copying adult behaviour as a way of rehearsing for a grown up life. Research indicates that pushchairs where the child faces the adult are better for communication development and strengthening the bond between adult and child as the baby has face to face contact which encourages early two-way communication.

When you take young babies for walks, visits and other outings in prams or pushchairs, encourage them to take a favourite cuddly toy with them such as a doll, teddy or animal. As you talk about what you can see, include the toy in the conversation as this gives a role model for the child to use in later activities when they take toys for walks in toy prams and pushchairs.

Heads Up, Lookers and Communicators

Babies will start to use small versions of all sorts of transport to begin taking their toys out and about with them. When going for a walk with an adult they are likely to ask to get out of the pushchair and love to help to push it – with a toy in it they can begin to learn about being careful in order to keep their 'baby' safe. They will quickly progress from this to using replica pushchairs for independent walks with their toys.

Sitters, Standers and Explorers

Young children (18-24 months)

Young children continue to enjoy using pushchairs and prams to take their toys for a walk. At this stage they are likely to need adult guidance to keep these on the pavement if walking along the street. In gardens and outdoor play areas they can practise in a safe and secure environment, becoming more skilled at negotiating obstacles and steering two, three and four wheeled vehicles such as carts, barrows, pushchairs, and trailers.

Movers, Shakers and Players

Children (24-36 months)

At this stage many children will start working together in 'mums, dads and babies' games which include using pushchairs for taking the babies out. These games encourage negotiating skills in the play as they decide who will have the pushchair and who will play each role - quite often the solution is that each child has a pushchair and baby as they play in parallel, so make sure you have more than one!

Walkers, Talkers and Pretenders

Foundation 1&2 (over 3)

As negotiation skills increase, and role play scenarios develop, the games become more complex and may include shopping, going to the doctor's or the clinic, the park or to visit other families. Pushchairs and any other means of transport will be included in the game and may become substitutes for cars or other vehicles. Linking indoor and outdoor play can encourage den making with empty packing cases, fabrics and other accessories.

Moving on into the Foundation Stage

Let's move it!

Babies and young children take delight in moving things from place to place. When they are very young they begin to realise things have gone, then they realise they can move things themselves, firstly with adult help, then independently or with their friends.

Young babies (0-8 months)

Very young babies start watching their parent/carers moving things when preparing for routines such as feeding and changing. At these times you could give them toys to hold and explore by moving them from hand to hand. Of course one way of making things move is to drop it, often repeatedly, so the adult can retrieve it for them! Simple rolling, pushing and pulling toys will also help babies realise their ability to make things move.

Heads Up, Lookers and Communicators

Babies (8-18 months)

Encourage babies to play with small toys with wheels. These can be moved across floor spaces indoor and outdoors as they begin to move themselves. Offer vehicles such as tractors, trailers, bulldozers in sand trays to move the sand from A to B. This is good preparation for them doing similar things with sit'n'ride toys. Some babies will get fascinated by the idea of moving things by filling bags or baskets and taking them somewhere else.

Sitters, Standers and Explorers

Young children (18-24 months)

If you provide wheeled toys with lift-up lids or trailer compartments, young children will fill them with toys, moving them from one place to another and then tipping them out. This is a key feature in making connections in their learning. Encourage them to repeat the exercise for putting the equipment away afterwards, and they will become even more proficient at the skill. You may need extra vehicles for this sort of play, so keep checking.

Movers, Shakers and Players

Children (24-36 months)

Encourage children to link the skill of moving resources with role play. Initially this is likely to involve taking babies or toys for walks, mimicking the adults who are special in their lives. If they are used to seeing adults moving other things for their work or in DIY, this may be how they include moving in role play. Remember to talk with the children about what they are doing in their play as this helps them to reinforce the learning and language.

Walkers, Talkers and Pretenders

Foundation 1&2 (over 3)

Children will build on the role play as they become more confident and aware of what goes on in the world. They also try to make sense of things for themselves, so at this stage take them to look at a building site or other workplace nearby where they will be able to re-enact the movement of bricks, mortar, scaffolding etc. by using wheeled vehicles and other 'movers' such as pulleys and ropes, barrows, buckets and trailers. Strong twine pulled over a wire can make a very simple pulley mechanism if actual pulleys are not available.

Moving on into the Foundation Stage

Passengers

Young children delight in pretending to be each other. Some wheeled vehicles make it easier to be parent and child, mother and father, older and younger siblings. An increasing number of tricycles and bicycles are designed for more than one child. Explore the possibilities of these for your setting.

Young babies (0-8 months)

Young babies enjoy watching others and following the movement with their eyes. If they are held by adults and encouraged to watch older children who are playing cooperatively on multi seat bicycles, they are more likely to join in when they are developmentally ready. You can also make moving fun by sitting on simple wheeled or stationary vehicles together and talking or singing about what you are doing.

Heads Up, Lookers and Communicators

Babies (8-18 months)

Babies will enjoy investigating the toys for two or more and seeing how the different parts work. They may sit and move the pedals around with their hands or sit on the seat and manipulate the handlebars in one direction or another. When they are able to sit confidently they will be able to ride on the vehicles as a passenger, usually with an older child as driver. The opportunities these toys give for conversations should be encouraged.

Sitters, Standers and Explorers

Young children (18-24 months)

As they become more confident on their feet, young children will be able to help propel the bikes and trikes by pushing their peers on them from front and back. You will need to stay close and watch to monitor what is happening. At this stage if the vehicles are the right size, the young children may be able to 'scoot' them along, possibly working together to do so. Look for cars and bikes that don't have pedals to make this easier.

Movers, Shakers and Players

Children (24-36 months)

Some children will be able to pedal <u>and</u> steer multi-person vehicles at this age depending on their physical development and ability to co-operate. Others will find it difficult and need lots of encouragement. Some of these bikes and trikes are quite heavy to manoeuvre, especially with more than one person on board, so they may find it easier to practice if their passengers are toys, at least to start with. Shop around for lighter versions of these toys.

Walkers, Talkers and Pretenders

Foundation 1&2 (over 3)

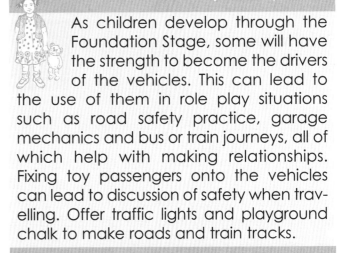

As children develop through the Foundation Stage, some will have the strength to become the drivers of the vehicles. This can lead to the use of them in role play situations such as road safety practice, garage mechanics and bus or train journeys, all of which help with making relationships. Fixing toy passengers onto the vehicles can lead to discussion of safety when travelling. Offer traffic lights and playground chalk to make roads and train tracks.

Moving on into the Foundation Stage

Trailers

Adding trailers to bikes, cars, tractors and trucks can extend their use for babies and young children to move things around. With trailers there is a wide range of activities from being transported and doing the transporting, depending on the age and stage of development of the child.

Young babies (0-8 months)

A young baby can lie in a trailer if it is of a suitable size and well padded. Then they can be gently transported by either an adult or older child under supervision. This way of travelling gives the sensation of being pulled which is different from being pushed. If the trailer has slatted sides, babies will also be able to see and hear through the sides of the trailer.

Heads Up, Lookers and Communicators

Babies (8-18 months)

As babies become more mobile and begin to investigate what is around them, they will climb in and out of trailers. This activity may need some adult support and involvement, and the experience will vary depending upon whether the trailer has four wheels so is flat, or has a tow bar and two wheels which will make it more difficult. Babies also love filling and emptying any container offered to them, so offer bricks, card cones, soft toys etc.

Sitters, Standers and Explorers

Young children (18-24 months)

Young children will love to climb in and sit in trailers, ready to be towed by peers who may need help from a sensitive adult. They will also try to tow the trailers themselves. At this stage children are likely to need help to steer as the task requires a combination of skill and strength. Try to offer vehicles without pedals at this age, leaving the children to propel the vehicle by foot along the ground.

Movers, Shakers and Players

Children (24-36 months)

As their muscle strength and coordination develop, you can introduce trailers that fix on pedalled toys. At this stage children will investigate how the pedals and the steering works and may need help to coordinate it all. Look at and talk about other transport with trailers such as container lorries, tractors, luggage trucks, Land Rovers. Add trailers to small wheeled vehicles so they can practice in miniature.

Walkers, Talkers and Pretenders

Foundation 1&2 (over 3)

Look together at the mechanisms for fixing trailers to the towing vehicles. Children will learn the different ways of joining them up themselves and spend time putting them together and separating them. Talk about how reversing and towing work by trying with small world vehicles such as tractors or cars with caravans. Watch vehicles reversing (from a safe distance) and see how the cab wheels turn to make the trailer move. Test the toys to see which works best, which is best for moving different sorts of loads or people.

Moving on into the Foundation Stage

Scooters

Scooters need good balance, good vision and strength to steer. They are very good for developing these skills and should be part of every setting. Make sure the scooters are of appropriate size and not too heavy. Explore all the different styles and types, and have some with three wheels, which will help the youngest children.

Very young babies will only really be able to watch as older children scoot past or round them. It's important to encourage the development of sounds and words as you talk with babies, so use the correct names for 'bike', 'scooter', 'barrow', 'pushchair', 'barrel' etc. Making silly sounds as bikes and scooters pass is also a good way to help babies develop control of their voices, tongues and teeth in preparation for talking.

Heads Up, Lookers and Communicators

As babies develop their muscles and can stand with help, stable wheeled toys such as scooters with three or four wheels will often be used as supports for pulling up to standing, or as a prop to moving along the ground. They also provide a flat surface for moving favourite toys or other objects. Help older babies to feel the movement by giving them little supported rides on three or four wheeled scooters indoors where there is a soft surface to fall on.

Sitters, Standers and Explorers

Young children (18-24 months)

At this stage, young children will really start to show independence in moving scooters and bikes. they may sit on a scooter and scoot with their feet, pull or push the scooter as they walk in front, behind or alongside, and some may begin to experiment with scooting in the regular way, particularly if someone shows them how to do it. Three and four wheeled scooters are still the best for this age, as they give a bit more stability.

Movers, Shakers and Players

Children (24-36 months)

Scooting will now become the preferred way of getting about for some children. However, it is not an easy skill to learn, and they need time and space to practice the specialised movements needed. However, it is a great activity to develop stamina, movement skill and concentration. Try tying streamers or strings of bells to scooter handles to make a focus and increase interest, or add a bike basket or shiny handlebar bell.

Walkers, Talkers and Pretenders

Foundation 1&2 (over 3)

By now, most children will be able to scoot well, and need some more challenges to keep their interest. Moving to two wheeled scooters is one way, or you could make obstacle courses with chalk, small cones, bean bags or skipping ropes, so the children can learn to manoeuvre between and around them. Tabards, hats or badges with 'Dispatch Rider' or 'Messenger' and bags for parcels and messages will spice up the rides on scooters and bikes. Older children could look for examples of other two wheeled vehicles in books and when out on walks.

Moving on into the Foundation Stage

33

Skates and skateboards

Skates and skateboards give an independent way of moving on wheels. Having wheels under your feet while standing may be a new and unusual feeling that takes some practice, but will be a great aid to helping babies and children improve their balance skills.

Young babies (0-8 months)

Very young babies may enjoy exploring a clean roller skate or skateboard, using hands and fingers. You could hold very young babies on the skateboard and push them along to give them an experience of riding and feeling air flow over their faces and through their hair. Watching and listening to older children on skates and boards will give good exercise for very young eyes and ears as they follow sounds and sights.

Heads Up, Lookers and Communicators

Babies (8-18 months)

Let the babies continue to investigate the workings of skates and skateboards. Encourage them to push the wheels around and feel the difference between metal and plastic wheels. They can push and pull the skates and skateboards backwards and forwards, or use them to give a favourite toy a ride. Help them to climb on board so they can have a little ride indoors or on the grass where tumbles can be managed safely.

Sitters, Standers and Explorers

Young children (18-24 months)

Scooting with one foot on a skate or a skateboard, over carpet to start with, will give the children an early experience of balancing while moving. As children develop confidence in standing and walking hold the young child on a skateboard and let them feel the sensation of standing and moving a very small amount. If a child is very confident hold on to the child and pull them along gently. Stay on a flat surface to start with.

Movers, Shakers and Players

Children (24-36 months)

Children's skates tend to be one of two kinds: wheels to attach to shoes with straps or mini roller boots. Plastic versions are safer and more pliable to use. As children become confident walkers you could get some beginner skates. Encourage children to investigate these in different ways and then help them put them on. Support them as they stand in them and, if they are happy, gently pull them along or encourage them to shuffle along.

Walkers, Talkers and Pretenders

Foundation 1&2 (over 3)

Children can explore how skates and skateboards work. They can push toys on them for rides and include them in their imaginative play. They will investigate how the wheels go round and how they are joined to the boots or board. Some children will be confident enough to skate or skateboard on their own, but must be carefully supervised. Trainers with wheels attached to the heel are now available as are roller blades which have a single row of wheels along the middle and work on a similar principle to ice skates. Try them all!

Moving on into the Foundation Stage

Rock and ride

The rocking motion is central to caring for babies and young children, rocking and swinging both stimulate brain growth. Practitioners should build this activity into their setting as a key movement experience, both in whole body rocking and in play experiences with rocking toys.

Young babies (0-8 months)

Many baby seats have a built in rocking motion, so when the baby is in them and fidgets the seat rocks naturally. They are also easy for adults to rock, but remember to use these carefully as babies need to be able to stretch their own arms and legs to practise large muscle movement. As young babies develop strength in their upper back and necks, you could hold them on rocking toys to feel the rocking motion.

Heads Up, Lookers and Communicators

Babies (8-18 months)

Using appropriate sized rocking horses or other animals, sit together on them, holding the babies so they can rock backwards and forwards with you. As you ride together, say appropriate rocking rhymes such as 'Ride a cock horse to Banbury Cross' or 'Row, Row, Row the Boat'. As they become used to the sensation and improve their balancing skills they may want to try to sit on their own with you in close proximity for safety.

Sitters, Standers and Explorers

Young children (18-24 months)

As children gain strength in their back and leg muscles, encourage them to climb on and off the rocking toys on their own as well as riding on their own. Talk to the young children about where they are going on their rides. Encourage them to lean backwards and forwards to adjust the speed of the motion. Play simple rocking games in pairs or groups, sitting on the floor and rocking gently backwards and forwards or from side to side.

Movers, Shakers and Players

Children (24-36 months)

Take children to parks where they are able to ride on the spring based rides which have bikes, boats or animals on them. This bouncing action is different and uses different muscles. As children gain confidence they will bounce on them more and lean in different directions to adjust the movement. Talk to the children about directions and speeds. Explore swinging as well, to continue the beneficial effect of these actions.

Walkers, Talkers and Pretenders

Foundation 1&2 (over 3)

As the children become older they can investigate the different types of movement mechanisms in rocking toys, swings and springs. Talk about different heights and speeds as well as what they look like. Discuss their preferences and why they like certain toys and movements. Encourage the children to design new rides or link them into obstacle courses. Look for pictures of swings, swingboats and other rides on the internet and in books.

Moving on into the Foundation Stage

How unusual!

If you look in toy catalogues and on websites you will find some exciting and quirky new sorts of ride-on vehicles for children. These include quad bikes, sit-on scooters, tyres, pogo sticks, trikes for lying or standing on, motor bikes and many others. These will add interest for children and give them new opportunities for moving in different ways.

Young babies (0-8 months)

If there is snow, take well-wrapped babies out and give them a tiny ride on a sledge. A similar experience can be re-enacted indoors as a follow up by using trays. Try out rides on other unusual wheeled or non-wheeled vehicles by exploring their potential for beginning riders.

Heads Up, Lookers and Communicators

Babies (8-18 months)

Use the new sorts of rides to continue to explore different ways of moving or being moved. Scooting along on a scooting toy which is intended for older children can be an exciting experience with the help of an adult. When there is snow sit a baby on an adult's lap and hold carefully as the adult and child travel on a sledge. Introduce this with a very slow and gentle ride to ensure that the baby is ready for this unusual experience.

Sitters, Standers and Explorers

Young children (18-24 months)

Look out for unusual rides for children as they grow, so they have new experiences as they grow and gain confidence. Add motor bikes, quad bikes etc. of suitable sizes. If and when it snows, encourage young children to push and pull sledges and/or trays across snow or sand. They may like to push their toys along on them to give them a ride or they could sit with their friends in the sledge and work together. Supervise carefully, as snow is now so rare.

Movers, Shakers and Players

Children (24-36 months)

Riding, rolling, sliding and scooting are all features of more unusual rides - try animals with wheels or rockers, big wheel bikes, plastic bases with superfast wheels, tyre toys etc. These will all extend the outdoor fun as children explore them together! As the children gain strength and confidence look at other types of rides to introduce if it snows. Snowmobiles and quad bikes could be introduced to children as now toys by riding with adults.

Walkers, Talkers and Pretenders

Foundation 1&2 (over 3)

At this stage children can experiment with making their own wheeled toys with your help. Offer tyres, boards, wheels and axles, drums, spools and steering wheels. Let children investigate all these features, and be around to help if they need it. Talk to them about simple home made designs such as go-karts. Encourage them to try to design and build one with adult help. They can talk about and draw designs for different ideas.

Moving on into the Foundation Stage

Existing and planned titles in the Baby and Beyond series include:

* **Messy Play** (ready now)
* **Sensory Experiences** (ready now)
* **Music and Sound** (ready now)
* **The Natural World** (ready now)
* **Construction** (ready now)
* **Marks & Mark Making** (ready now)
* **Dolls and Soft Toys** (ready now)

* **Bikes, Prams & Pushchairs** (ready)
* **Cooking** (2007)
* **Finger Songs and Rhymes** (2007)
* **Small World Play** (2007)
* **Stories, Songs, Rhymes** (2007)
* **Counting** (2008)
* **Role Play** (2008)